TRIUMPH HOUSE
Poetry with a Purpose

HAPPY DAYS

Edited by

CHRIS WALTON

First published in Great Britain in 1998 by
TRIUMPH HOUSE
1-2 Wainman Road, Woodston,
Peterborough, PE2 7BU
Telephone (01733) 230749

All Rights Reserved

Copyright Contributors 1998

HB ISBN 1 86161 480 2
SB ISBN 1 86161 485 3

FOREWORD

Whether going away or staying close to home, summer strikes a chord in all of us.

Childhood holidays, faraway lands and the beauty of the countryside are just a few of the many topics covered in *'Happy Days'*.

Over one hundred poets have joined together to create an anthology full of fun, laughter and joy that will cheer and uplift any reader.

Chris Walton
Editor

Contents

Seashore	Nona Lewis	1
My Brother - Wet Behind The Ears	Carol Prior	2
Monte Carlo	Janet Jones	3
Lake Michigan	Jean Calver	4
My Secret Place	Danielle A Evans	5
A Jewel In God's Worldly Crown	Elaine Hawkins	6
Upon The Moors	Keith L Powell	7
Hello	Margaret Elliott Woods	8
Paradise Island	Samantha Ferranti	9
Sunshine Poem	Amy Barrett	10
The Place To Be In Summer	Fay Smith	11
Wishful Thinking	Sheila Thompson	12
The Fullness Of Summer	Jeannette Facchini	13
Windmills	Evelyne A McMaster	14
The Cornish Man	Janet Cavill	15
My Favourite Haunt	Dorothy Schofield	16
Funny Sights	Wendy Watkin	17
A Garden In Time	S'arabrab	18
Hidden Hamlet In The Vale	Gerald Aldred Judge	19
Postcard From Provence	Rita Douglas	20
Fife	J Scroggie	21
Mediterranean Magic	Pat Heppel	22
Holiday Delight	P M Wardle	23
Musings Of Summer	June F Allum	24
A Leafy Stroll	S Mullinger	25
Summertime In Brampton Park	Peter James O'Rourke	26
It's Summer	Nola B Small	27
If I Had Three Wishes . . .	Maria-Christina	28
Sunny Days	Julie Mckenzie	29
Dreams	Olive Irwin	30
Cornwall	Joan Hands	31
Scarborough	Evelyn Balmain	32
The Instinct (Not) To Travel	Claire-Lyse Sylvester	33
Sojourn	Nigel David Evans	34

Singing A Joyous Sound	Rosemary Medland	35
Garden Sun	Sarah Louise Morris	36
Holiday	Michael Bellerby	37
Barbados	Sue Gutteridge	38
The Seaside	Joy Benford	39
Paradise	Anisha Paddam	40
My Favourite Place	Helga I Dharmpaul	41
Holiday Memories	M Smith	42
Oakwood Park	David Eastmond James	43
Seaside Fun	Barbara Pearce	44
Heaven Is . . .	Elizabeth Mark	45
My Dream Holiday	Mary Ryan	46
Jolly	Paul Duddles	47
My Beloved Island	Marnie Connley	48
Tummel Valley	Sean McFadden	49
Our Favourite Place To Be	Merilyn Gulley	50
The Sea	Shirley	51
Summer	Peter Buss	52
Biased View	Edward J Butler	53
Singing The Song Of Jasmine	Norman Royal	54
Totnes, Devon	Maisie Dance	55
A Favourite Place	Irene Locke	56
Seaside Morning - Lowestoft, Suffolk	Walter Gilder	57
When The Sun Shines	Pamela A Smith	58
Where I'd Like To Be	Sharon Davies	59
Holidays	Joanna Mogford	60
Bank Holidays	Irene Carter	61
Home Ground	D A Watson	62
Summer Moment	Betty Tindal	63
My Garden	Susan B Marlow	64
A Tropical Dream	Terry White	65
Brancaster Beach, North Norfolk	Anita Richards	66
The River At Cambridge	Thelma Hynes	67
Holidays	Karen Jones	68
Where I Love To Be	Dorothy Whitehall	69
A Late Summer Afternoon	James Slater	70

Sussex	Marion P Webb	71
Caribbean Calypso	Christopher Johnson	72
Bonnie Scotland	M Muirhead	73
The Beauty Of Beaches	C Shadwell	74
The Land Of The Portuguese	Ada Ferguson	75
Holidays	Archie Grant	76
Dream Holiday	Mary Skelton	77
The Smell Of Summer	C J Walls	78
Summertime	Natalie Coleman	79
Wish You Were Here	John Hope Urwin	80
Holidays	Jane V Johnson	81
The Garden Centre	Jessica Wright	82
At The Seaside -Skegness	Michael John Swain	83
Dawn In A Summer Meadow	Janet Allen	84
Nant Y Moch	Wendy Dedicott	85
Paradise In The Summer	Kerry Hayley	86
Summertime	Katherine Ring	87
Colours Of The West	H McQuirke	88
Safe Haven For The Spiritual Warrior . . .	Arion	89
Korcula: Vistas Of A Dalmation Holiday	Anne Sanderson	90
The Celtic Prince	Elaine Carter	91
Eastbourne	Anne Clark	92
Joys Of Summer	Margaret Jackson	94
Sunny Hunny (Hunstanton)	Margery English	95
I'd Rather Be	Leanne Hall	96
Summer's Day	Dorothea Carroll	97
Mediterranean Medallion	Heather A Hayne	98
Childhood Memory	Lorraine Johns	99
Old Binoculars	Jacquie L Smith	100
Woodland Ramble	Peter Morriss	101
Kent In Summer	Joanne Manning	102
Woodland Garden	Yvonne Wilkinson	103

Seashore

Exhilarating feeling,
                as you walk along the beach,
You feel the sand beneath your feet,
                the sea's within your reach.
You feel the breeze so gentle,
                as it ruffles up your hair,
Your steps begin to quicken
                for you haven't got a care.
The rippling waves of green and blue
                that break upon the shore
Invite you to partake of them,
                you could not ask for more.
And so at last you get to where
                the sand and water meet,
You step into those blissful waves -
                refreshed, restored, replete.

Nona Lewis

MY BROTHER - WET BEHIND THE EARS

Burying your sister
Is a good old seaside game,
But when it comes to his turn
The fun's just not the same.

So when I got my own back
He didn't find it funny,
'Oh come on I can't get out
I'll give you all my money.'

I didn't move to help him
He's always such a pain,
If I give in and dig him out
He'll annoy me once again.

It was only minutes later
When a dog came very near,
He sniffed my brother, cocked his leg
And tiddled in his ear.

I couldn't help for laughing
And it woke my dad and mum,
I'd grabbed the camera quickly
To preserve my seaside fun.

Mum and Dad were not amused
They said it wasn't fair,
But I'll never forget that look on his face
And the wet patch in his hair.

Carol Prior

MONTE CARLO

Oh to be in Monte Carlo
Where the sky seems ever blue,
Scorching sun and glistening water
- Flowers of every shade and hue.

See the grand yachts in the harbour,
And the crystal glass, and wine
Set upon the polished table
Ready for the rich to dine.

Hear the waves that gently ripple
On the boats securely moored,
While the famous laze and sunbathe
Always smart and never bored!

See the palace in the sunlight
In its splendour, gleaming white.
In the clock tower chimes are sounding
Filling tourists with delight.

High above the great casino
Watch the setting sun go down,
Waiting for the well-dressed gamblers
Coming in from out of town.

Step inside and see the grandeur
Wonder if it's truly real,
As the millionaires arriving
Come to play the roulette wheel.

Through the night they play the table
Until they're sure that they have won.
- Oh to be in Monte Carlo
In the heat of noonday sun!

Janet Jones

LAKE MICHIGAN

As I sit beneath the azure sky,
I just prayed for the sun to shine.
Lake Michigan called me yet again
No crowds, this place I call mine.
There are nature trails to walk
When the sun dies down,
Be careful for the insects bite,
When day turns into night.
This place in the States is tranquillity
With its stretch of pale blue water
I seem to unwind with each passing day,
And return each year because I want to.
I enjoy the wildlife, and flowers
The culture so diverse
I meet so many interesting people
With whom I like to converse.
Two weeks flies by and it's time to leave,
Photos never do it justice,
But as winter approaches my memory tells me
The fishing I still have to practise.

Jean Calver

MY SECRET PLACE

My favourite place in the summer,
Is under a tree beside a river,
The beautiful green leaves,
Shade me from the scorching sun,
The oxygen from the leaves
is pure and clean and flows around me

The river is cool,
So I dangle my legs over the bank,
My toes are just touching the water,
The tiny ripples flow over my feet,
Trout dance just beneath the surface,
It's getting late, the sun's gone in
I shiver slightly as a cool breeze passes through the air,
I love this place, I'll be back tomorrow.

Danielle A Evans (13)

A Jewel In God's Worldly Crown

Amidst the company of forestry trees,
shaded by woodland, I lay in rich green ferns,
listening to the songs of the wind,
carried as soothing melodies on a soft summer's breeze,
watching the sun, as she sprays flecks of spun gold down,
shimmering they dance as spectral visions,
upon rustling leaves full of graceful intent.
I savour the scent of fallen bark and moss,
pine needles and dried withered brown leaves.
Their mingled odours linger fragrancing the warm air,
with pleasure I invite the scent to fill my nostrils.
Peace overwhelms me, easing me into an oblivious serenity,
Causing the pang of emotion, that creates longings and wishes,
I feel my wish, wanting to stay here, encapsulated,
in this moment, this place, forever,
Where I can never go back, or beyond now,
such is this overwhelming instant that drives me, to forget,
that I, could ever have existed, anywhere else,
in the world, except here.
As insects perform their daily grind,
I lay down my troubles, hiding from one reality,
only to find another, so much more pleasing,
I succumb to this natural beauty, loitering peacefully,
within this place, I envision to be, set as a jewel,
so perfectly within God's worldly crown,
Until burns orange the setting sun, all around me,
its rays reach out, to cover this place in a chiffon haze.
I stay, watching this blissful moment fade to its end,
before returning to my other, less than pleasing reality.

Elaine Hawkins

UPON THE MOORS

I like to be upon the moors high up so far away
In the summer when there is much to see
I can walk for miles without a care
Just miles and miles in the nice clean air.

I like to be upon the moors high up so far away
Lots of cattle and sheep do I see
A sheep dog or two comes near me
Panting too because it is hot
It is so clear with the view I have got.

I like to be upon the moors high up so far away
Taking me away from the town where I have to stay
But here there is no people or any rush
I can find the time, time enough on such a nice clear day
It is a shame I am going home today
Back to a placc I hate with people of a mixed-up hate
Until I can come back again next year.

Keith L Powell

HELLO

Thought I'd let you know
Weather here is great
Had a day with poorly tum
Just something I ate!

Late nights, sleeping in
Having hordes of fun
There's always so much to do
Something for everyone.

It's still my favourite place
Soft sand and gentle breezes
Then there's that cool night air
Brings me a few sneezes.

Everywhere the eye can see
Flowers' bold bright colours
They bloom so big and beautiful
With a perfume like no other.

I have the sound of the waves
Warmth of the sunshine
And such peace
There is no other place for me

Than the beauty and magic
                     of Greece.

Love
Mags

Margaret Elliott Woods

PARADISE ISLAND

Azure, turquoise seas
That sparkle in the golden sun
Pale, white sandy beaches
With tall tropical palm trees
Blowing in the light sea breeze.

Seagulls softly fly across the ripples of the ocean,
Splashes from dolphins disturbing the inky blue seas
Crafty crabs drift onto the pale sands
A paradise island is a heavenly summer's day.

Samantha Ferranti (11)

SUNSHINE POEM

Nothing suits me better
On a lovely summer's day
Than to saunter round our garden
In a very relaxing way.

We don't find it hard to find a loo
Or a space to sit down for a cup of tea
Or a meal for two;
But we can just walk in
And get what we fancy
And do what we want to do.
This is what we call
A holiday for two.

I am not able to sit in the sun
Otherwise I would get burnt up like a bun
A shady place suits me best
Where I can just lie back and rest.

We potter about in our garden
It's just like being on the shore
Home is the place for us
Could you ask for more?

Amy Barrett

THE PLACE TO BE IN SUMMER

People come from round the globe
In August every year
To Edinburgh to see the shows
And soak up the atmosphere.

All the performers spread out
Along The Royal Mile
Three hundred actors strut their stuff
And do it well with style.

Jugglers, acrobats and rubber men
Hold their audience in suspense
If you enjoy the acts you see
Contribute a few pence.

Shakespeare music and comedy
All types of turns have their place
As each performer does his act
In his allotted space.

The crowds mull round to watch
Beneath the summer sun
They clap and cheer and compliment
A piece of work well done.

Stalls with craft-work are displayed
Paintings and the arts
'Poems and Pints' to entertain
And books of many sorts.

The atmosphere is electric
People so friendly and free
No words can express the experience
You have to be there - to see.

Fay Smith

WISHFUL THINKING

I was asked where I would like to be,
on a sunny summer's day,
Well! I shall tell you because,
if I had my way,
I would like to swim, and float,
in the deep blue sea until it's time for tea,
then laze in a deck chair,
an ice cream in my hand.
Not for me the promenade,
or the sound of a big brass band.
I would like a quiet companion,
I do have someone on my mind,
he is nice and gentle,
and very, very kind.
We like the same sort of music,
as long as it's not too loud,
away from the 'madding crowd',
It is not too much to ask for,
the sandy beach, deck chairs and sea,
with someone who loves me.

Sheila Thompson

THE FULLNESS OF SUMMER

Thank you for a day that sings of summer
From an earth that shouts 'beauty, glory'
                            to her Maker.
Thank you for colours that lift and thrill
Bringing joy, gladness and peace to the heart,
This is how it should be,
It feels so right.
You made summer to be like this,
This was your plan -
        The fullness of summer.

Jeannette Facchini

WINDMILLS

I hear the 'swish' of the sails,
And of the river, rippling by,
But the windmills claim, a special sight,
Under and clear and cloudless sky.

The Kinderdijk mills stand on the hill,
Majestic, and so tall,
Guarding well surrounding lands,
And watching, over all.

Like an 'X' the sails reach out,
To welcome you and me,
Who come to visit in summertime,
Then, have a cup of tea!

But they send the sails a'racing,
When the east wind blows so strong,
Spinning like a carousel,
'Neath clouds that race along.

Evelyne A McMaster

THE CORNISH MAN

Today I'm going to Cornwall
St Ives to be precise,
I'll go by train - the Cornish Man,
Will bear me on my way.

I'll walk and swim,
I'll eat and sleep,
I'll relax and I shall bathe
On a lovely Cornish beach my dear
I'll hold you close to me.

On glorious summer evenings
I'll wile away the time
I'll visit ancient churches
To thank God for these days.

I'll walk along the sea front
And hold on to your arm
I'll get to know you sweet one
I'll love you with my heart.

We've had a lovely wedding day
My darling one and I
Today's the day we speak of 'we'
and never more of 'I'.

Today we stood before God's altar
We must never, never falter.

Janet Cavill

MY FAVOURITE HAUNT

When the temperature reaches eighty three,
I know where I'd rather be,
Not sheltering under a shady tree,
Sipping delicious ice-cool tea.
But high upon the south Pennine moors,
That wild beautiful great outdoors,
Listening to the skylark's pure notes
Bursting joyfully from its small throat,
As up and up it soars so high,
Into the blue of a summer sky.
Cold crystal clear waters of moorland streams
Go tumbling down forever it seems,
Down, down, down,
Towards the distant smudge of the town.
Breathing deeply the pure clear air,
Time stands still as I sit and stare
At all this beauty surrounding me
And it's all absolutely free.
The summer breeze sighs through cotton grass,
And pretty white flowers dance en masse.
Up here my ancestors' farms once stood,
Their love of the moors runs through my blood.
I imagine them going about daily tasks
Until sunset time and day is past.
The only sounds are the bleating of sheep,
And the slithering sliding noise of my feet
As I scramble down the packhorse tracks,
Time to head home, but soon I'll be back.

Dorothy Schofield

FUNNY SIGHTS

Summer days brightly glow,
Beaches beckon,
'Shall we go?'
Let's take sandwiches
and make it a day
Providing the weather
keeps OK.
'Don't forget the sun cream,'
We must not burn.
Some poor people
never learn.
Glowing like beetroots,
why don't they think
Instead of peeling,
and turning pink?
Some funny sights,
You often see,
Flabby stomachs,
Knobbly knees,
Bald heads like beacons,
Should have worn a hat.
She's wearing shorts
but is much too fat.
Never mind, they want a tan,
must expose,
as much as they can.
This way, that way
There they go
Wibble, wobble,
To and fro.

Wendy Watkin

A Garden In Time

Like ladies of a bygone age
Amid the parsley and the sage
In knot design or green parterre
I dream that I am walking there
Inside the walls of good red brick
I gather herbs that 'do the trick'.

Unlike the girls of yesteryear
No crinolines and bonnets here
But in our love of garden lore
We walk in jeans and hat of straw
To gather as they've always done
The green herbs ripened in the sun

Secure inside my garden's wall
I glory in the flowers all
And as I move from here to there
I marvel at the earth, so fair,
Whose one desire it seems to me
Is beautifying all we see.

The calm and peace and joy it lends
To jaded spirit and nerve-ends
Is balm to mind and body too
In our fast world of 'rush' and 'do'.
So meditate, and so renew
The soul, as our ancestors knew

Like ladies of a bygone age
Amid the parsley and the sage
A garden's such a heavenly place
To walk and watch the flowers grace
The earth with beauty and with scent
And contemplate the years that went.

S'arabrab

HIDDEN HAMLET IN THE VALE
(For Aidan)

Here a journey may take forever
yet folk never wander far away.
Here earth is our mother and from her
clouds soiled by no city ever stray,
born of the adoration of life
spirit of the waterfalls display.
Here no one hangs a line of washing
over someone else's sunny day,
far from city legal trickery
here that which you take you must repay,
though many have often sought the vale
few have ever found or known the way,
for the path is within your own heart
there the remnants of 'hidden vale' lay . . .

Gerald Aldred Judge

POSTCARD FROM PROVENCE

Far above the azure sea
Dazzling in the sun and haze,
Looking down to the town below
Palm trees wafting in the breeze.

This is a painter's paradise
Colours so sharp and bright,
Red tiles in their vivid shades,
Bring a picture of delight.

The corniche lit up high above
With twinkling fairy lights,
Yachts bobbing in the harbour
Warm, magical, balmy nights.

The fragrance of the orange trees
Is perfume in the air,
This little bit of Provence
There's none that can compare.

Worshipped from the olden days
You have your grace and flair
Colourful, vibrant, all aglow
Give me a wish and I'll be there.

Rita Douglas

FIFE

Sun on the hill,
Wind in the grass,
Can we surmount
this indomitable pass.

But it's not on the ordinary
physical plane. It's of mind
and of spirit and things
we can't tame.

Still a walk in the forest
that once was an old haunt,
In the kingdom of Fife
by stream and trout loch.

My mind now slips back
to those primitive days,
With logs on the fire
and friends that would stay.

Heaven was my mantle
with myriads of stars.
My heart is still fain
for that northerly star.

J Scroggie

MEDITERRANEAN MAGIC

Masts on leisure yachts standing high,
Striped funnels on cruise ships 'gainst an azure sky,
Plump oranges nestling amongst so-green leaves,
The crystal sea wafting a welcome breeze,
These are the delights of the Mediterranean!

High rugged coastlines, desolate and bare
Hugging sandy bays - only boats can get there!
Tall conifers hiding a hoard of cones,
Minute vivid flowers between tumbled stones,
These are the beauties of the Mediterranean!

Swimming pools twinkling periwinkle blue,
Lots of leisure time, so little to do.
Skimpily-clad bodies bronzing to copper,
Enjoying the freedom such holidays offer,
This is the lure of the Mediterranean!

Ancient monuments and places read about in books,
Cathedrals and churches worth a second look.
Villages and hamlets away from civilisation,
Islands, the treasures of many different nations,
These are the jewels of the Mediterranean!

Happy holidaymakers soaking up the sun,
Children on white beaches having lots of fun.
Long cool drinks beneath a parasol's shade,
The icy tingling when taking a bathe,
These are my memories of the Mediterranean!

Pat Heppel

HOLIDAY DELIGHT

Oh such delight to be here
On such a lovely day
The sun is hot and I see
The children play
The breeze is cool on my skin
The sun beating down
How delighted that I am here
Taking all the sun
A holiday of delight
I have waited for so long
But now I am on my own
Sitting on this beach
Yes I miss Bill and Jack
But I know now when I return
I don't want either back.

P M Wardle

MUSINGS OF SUMMER

These words, so full of cheer,
Really wish that you were here.
The sun is bright, the birds in song,
Distantly church bells, go ding, dong!
As I walk past a babbling brook,
At nature's beauty so pleased to look.
Wooded glade and trees, with boughs outstretched,
Just calling the artist to be sketched.
Perhaps will come a shower of rain,
Clean and sweet the air smells again.
Children playing happily in the park,
People walking their dogs, with joy they bark.
Busy roads, crowded shops, life's one bustle,
During the day it is all hustle.
As evening draws nigh, all is serene,
Birds, bees, and flowers, on village green.
Many folk will travel far and wide,
The place I love best, the British countryside.

June F Allum

A Leafy Stroll

A walk in the woods, fills me with pleasure,
In summer I can stride out at leisure.
No sunbathing at the nearest beach for me,
But visits to the woods, for a walk among trees.
Shadows on paths, overhead canopy,
Means rambling in coolness, the place to be.
Flowers dancing at large tree bases please,
Bustling leaves create a refreshing breeze.
Walking in woods, a pleasant sensation,
Summer strolls made without perspiration.

S Mullinger

SUMMERTIME IN BRAMPTON PARK

Where butterflies with love enhance
And worthy of remark,
Perform for me their summer dance
In peaceful Brampton Park.

A dance of love, a dance of charm
Pure summertime delight,
Like hearts released in joyful calm,
Souls fly before my sight.

Where rays of sunshine kiss the rose
And beauty senses seize,
It's Brampton Park in summer pose
Caressed by fragrant breeze.

While bees achieve in harmony
With wonder to amaze,
And swaying trees bow gracefully,
Love's beating heart of praise.

A tranquil place for thought and dream
Where squirrels play and climb,
And blackbirds sing in high esteem,
In praise of summertime.

Where nature holds my heart and mind
And beauty shows her face,
She holds me with her spell to bind,
In summertime embrace.

Peter James O'Rourke

IT'S SUMMER

It's summer, it's summer
When we all rush to the beach.
It's summer, it is when
we get our legs pulled by
        sharks.
It's summer, it's summer
When we all shower under
        the sprinkler
It's summer, it is
When the wasps bathe in our
        spilt juice.
Yes, it's summer when Gramps
        goes windsurfing.
It's summer, it's summer
When we fight for a cold lollipop
        or Coke.
It's summer, it's summer when we
want to sleep in the freezer.
It's summer, it's summer
It's hot, hot, hot!
It's summer, it's summer,
        Is it not?

Nola B Small

IF I HAD THREE WISHES . . .

If I had three wishes, first I would choose
A Star Trek transporter, to travel the world.
So I could *really* choose a favourite place!
But meanwhile I love

Awesome Arizona
The Grand Canyon State,
With lofty palm trees, majestic mountains,
Superb sunshine, and *space!*
And such wonders as Petrified Forest,
Painted Desert, Meteor Crater, Tucson's Desert Museum,
The film studios with oh-so-skilful stuntmen,
Rodeos, chuck-wagon suppers,
Cactus forest, with mighty Saguaro cacti,
Period-piece Tombstone,
Bizarre Boot Hill,
Spectacular Sedona, with red cliffs and Mystic Hills.

Good food, friendly hospitable people -
Hunky John Wayne lookalikes
And much, much more - any wonder that
I love *amazing Arizona?*

Maria-Christina

SUNNY DAYS

I love to be by the water
on a hot and sweaty summer's day,
For there a gentle breeze is blowing
that keeps the heat at bay.

I love to walk in the country
seeing all things anew under sun's light,
For then the view can be seen clearly
and what a wonderful sight!

I thank God for the sunshine,
it fills our hearts with glee,
I am glad there's no rain in heaven,
just sunshine for all eternity!

Julie Mckenzie

DREAMS
(For Mom and Dad)

The sea air flowing through my hair,
The sound of the waves on the rocks,
The sound of my heartbeat in my ears,
The sand at my feet
The spray of water hitting my legs,
Seashells in my hands,
Footprints in the sand
Caused by children, sandcastles build.
I remember my childhood dreams.

Olive Irwin

CORNWALL

Peninsular of fire
lit by ancient days,
beautiful Cornwall
we fall for thee.
Soft timeless valleys
up-dale, down-dale
legends unwind
glorious seascapes
to find,
fairies in glens
count all the blessings
this island sends.

Joan Hands

SCARBOROUGH

Town of gardens fresh and green,
Hills rising breathless, high,
Sea pounding shore in ceaseless tides,
Gulls soaring in the sky.

The Spa in grey stone splendour
From past to present brought,
Victorian buildings in array
Imagination caught.

Ponds, parks, and arbours hiding
At pathways' end we found.
Folks friendly, accents broad and warm,
Philosophy profound.

Scarboro' is popular still
In spite of modern times,
So we prefer to travel there
And not to foreign climes!

Evelyn Balmain

THE INSTINCT (NOT) TO TRAVEL

Behind closed bedroom curtains
The sun's playing hide-and-seek,
Using leafy branches for its early morning game -
Now you see me, now you don't; wake up!
Go downstairs, start the day
By admiring the view - breathtaking!
Green grass, tall trees . . . on the left,
Very near - an imposing beech; stretching . . .
Casting restless shadows on the ground. Mingling . . .
With two sweet-chestnut trees -
Busy producing long, thin,
Powdery flowers. Love them! Love them!
Tall trees higher than the house
I am in; so much higher than me.
Birds are singing; flying to and fro; stopping . . .
To drink - or bathe - in a weathered
Concrete bird bath. I am spellbound. Paradise!
Not far from the patio window I see a small pond,
Surrounded by a curvy flower-bed.
I see a terracotta jug nearby; a small pot -
Both begging to be dipped
In a cool, cool water
Waiting for wildlife to approach; thirstily . . .
On this midsummer's day. It's peaceful here.
I like it here. Terracotta pots, more terracotta pots,
Overflowing with colourful begonias; variegated ivy.
Colourful begonias; lobelias - a touch of blue!
Blue as the sky above
me; blue as the sky. Sweet moment . . .
Gentle loveliness. This . . . is home!

Claire-Lyse Sylvester

Sojourn

Riding on a train of thought,
Past summer field and fishing port,
To Bettws-y-Coed and Swallow Falls,
Where waters ripple and blackbirds call.

Is this where I stood so long ago
Before life's gusts and squalls and snow?
Now those childhood times are lost,
Forever swirled and thrown and tossed.

And yet in my mind's eye I stay,
To enjoy that summer's day,
And for a moment time holds fast,
In those days of dreams now past.

Nigel David Evans

SINGING A JOYOUS SOUND

I dream of being away
somewhere quiet and cool
on this scorching hot day
with you paddling in the pool.

Take your bucket and your spade
we'll make sandcastles in the sand
then when the picnic's ready-laid
will eat sandwiches holding your hand.

We'll pack away
and on the swings will ride.
Come let's play,
I love you with pride.

Now the ice cream van rings his bell.
Two lollies please,
lick it quick and I'll not tell
Mummy, you're a little tease.

Bring your ball in the park
we'll kick it around
until it's nearly dark
then go home singing a joyous sound.

I can't wait
please come again, we'll play in the sun.
Don't disappoint and don't be late.
Oh, being a granny is so much fun!

Rosemary Medland

GARDEN SUN

In the garden with a hose
Water trickling between my toes
This is where I love to be
When the sun shines down on me.

For in my garden so cool and calm
I am covered by summer's charm.
For this is where my dreams come true -
The place that stops me feeling blue,
As here the sun makes my skin so warm
While I lie sunbathing on the lawn.
Surrounded in peace and all alone
In a stress and work-free zone.

So I long for the summer sun
For when it comes so does fun
As I can go and be free
In my garden of fantasy.

Sarah Louise Morris

HOLIDAY

I would like to go to Spain
just for a week or two
To feel my feet in sand
and splash in waters blue.
I could lie there in the sun
and get the perfect tan,
Its healing power is awesome
and I'm its greatest fan.
A happy carefree time,
children laugh and play
A break from humdrum life,
never far away.
It matters not how far you go
as long as you unwind
Daft shorts, big hat, flip-flops too
no one seems to mind.
Postcards, photos, a small souvenir,
a bag of candy floss
It's my idea of heaven
two weeks without my boss.
But I'll savour every minute
for soon a memory it will be
Then I've only fifty weeks more saving
'til I'm back by the sea.

Michael Bellerby

BARBADOS

I mostly remember the Caribbean,
It was my ultimate dream.
Knowing that when I hit the 'big forty',
On its exotic beach I must be seen.
Soaking up the sweet hot sun,
Stroking the silky soft sand
This to me was a piece of paradise,
A truly romantic and magical land.
Evenings you could hear the tree frogs,
Smell the scent of the evening dew
Spend the night chatting round the pool,
And fresh pina coladaos I sunk quite a few.
Yes I remember when I hit that age of forty,
And I savour it with quite a smile.
I had the fortune to live my dream,
And I'll hang on to that smile quite a while.

Sue Gutteridge

THE SEASIDE

Down on the beach
gazing at the sea
that is where I'd
much rather be.
Going for a walk
along the sand
talking to my partner
as he holds my hand.
Feeling the breeze
just kissing my hair
I'll close my eyes
and pretend I am there.

Joy Benford

PARADISE

I long to be far away
From this place called home.
I'd like to sit by the sea
Underneath the warm sunshine.
On the white sand
Is where I long to be.
Eating coconuts from the nearby trees
In the hot summer sun.
At night I'd walk across the beach
And wish upon a star in the clear sky.
Far away in my sunny paradise
Is where I long to be.

Anisha Paddam (14)

My Favourite Place

As dawn is breaking,
Birds are awakening,
Greet the rays of the sun.
Gorse is still blooming.
Bunnies start grooming.
The day has begun.

The clouds are drifting,
As mist is lifting
From the land and the sea.
Mountain tops dreaming,
Lochens are gleaming,
It's heaven for me.

Heatherbells ringing,
Birds are now singing.
Welcome to the new day.
A breeze is blowing.
Flowers are showing.
Gone away the night's grey.

The deer is a-grazing,
The midday sun blazing.
To life: peace be with you.
Kneeling down, praying.
Trees around swaying,
As my vows I renew.

It's here, I belong.
My love is so strong
For you, Scottish Highlands,
All through the seasons,
Love is my reason.
The Highlands are my lands.

Helga I Dharmpaul

HOLIDAY MEMORIES

Looking through my album of holidays far and near
All were spent so happy with sometimes a little tear
Holidays with our children and dog, off we would go
Always to the seaside in a caravan we would roam
First it was Arbroath to the Lion Caravan Park
Playing on the beach and fairgrounds takes my memories back
Then it was to Saltcoat's sands and golden dunes
There we played so happy even the sun shone that June
Off next to Ayr the land of Rabbie Burns
Rained almost every day but still we had good fun
Holidays to Largs, Dunoon, Anstruther too
Now the children are adults, little dog gone
Off on a visit to London, was the Queen's Jubilee
Then off to Dover, took a ferry across the sea
Spent time in Germany, Ricky, just you and me
Then holidays spent at Whitley Bay, Scarborough, Margate too
Even over to Guernsey what a lovely view
There were many others that you and I have done
Then it was time to leave me as your life on earth was done
How I felt so lonely now there is only one
Took myself a cruise on Canberra made lots of new friends
Then with my daughter and grandson enjoying my holidays again
Off again on holiday my daughter grandson and me
Just like old times again playing by the sea
Then came other holidays more grandchildren too
Although I had a lovely time Ricky I still miss you
Looking through my albums at holidays that have past
Have left me happy memories I know will always last.

M Smith

OAKWOOD PARK

I like to go to Oakwood Park,
It is the place to have a lark,
I go there in the summertime
and drink lemon and lime.

'Mega-Fobia', the best ride around,
Makes your stomach hit the ground.

Help! you scream on 'Vertigo',
Makes your head go high and low.
So Oakwood Park is the place to be,
When your summertime is free.

David Eastmond James (11)

SEASIDE FUN

The water glistened with the sun
As it rose over the tranquil sea.
There was something near of a breeze
That brought home the salty air to me.

I was surrounded by my friends
Whose faces were covered in large smiles;
For this was the place to escape
From just another night on the tiles.

We spent days lying on the beach
With big ice creams and cold drinks galore.
Yet time had no meaning for us
We just wanted to relax some more.

The long nights were spent on the pier
Enjoying all the treats or a ride.
But one more chance to be a child
Will always run away like the tide.

Barbara Pearce

HEAVEN IS . . .

A Cornish cove, the sea and sky dream-blue.
So carefully planned, our holiday-for-two.
A B&B two minutes from the beach.
Olde-worlde shops almost within arms' reach.
A dairy selling clotted cream. Cool caves
To cuddle in. Beyond, white foaming waves.

In truth, right now, I'm sitting in my flat.
Outside, the rain pelts down, drip-drop, split-splat.
But any moment soon, he will arrive.
Hold me heart close, and later, we will drive
Through flower-fringed lanes, each tricky twist and bend
will bring us ever nearer to wild, wonderful
         Land's End!

Elizabeth Mark

MY DREAM HOLIDAY

I had a dream, a dream bizarre, that found me floating through
The office of a publisher I'd posted poems to.
And in the inner sanctuary, director there I saw,
I think he was called Ian, but of this I'm not too sure.

He was busy planning outing to please his motley crew,
Tired of stuffy offices, they'd felt it was their due.
His finger was firm-planted on a place on map of world,
Which from a dusty corner had remained too long unfurled.

E'en as I watched, his finger moved, economy in mind,
A less expensive holiday than Caribbean find.
Alighted on the Isle of Wight, more suited to his taste,
To spend too much on such a scheme would surely be a waste.

Then to the outer offices he made his measured tread,
To give the weary editors, still bleary from their bed,
To Heather, Steve and Andy, Chris and Suzy too,
The details of the outing of which they'd had but few.

He thought that they could hire a boat on Solent would be sound,
Heather manning anchor and, so not to run aground,
Chris and Andy take the wheel and steer a careful course,
Whilst Steve and Suzy brush up on the rudiments of Morse.

As would-be poet seeking oft' their much-prized recognition,
In my dream I thought I'd try and join their expedition.
But when I asked if I could come, be with them on the boat,
Not too surprised when I received one more rejection note.

Mary Ryan

JOLLY

A paddle in the cooling sea
Warm sand between my toes
Sunshine upon my pale legs
Deck chairs in a row
Distant screams of flying gulls
Laughter from the funfair
Kids riding friendly donkeys
While parents stand and stare
A trip upon the waterway
A boat so slowly cruising
Money spent in fruit machines
Not winning only losing
A walk along a windswept prom
A few ends of crown green bowls
A round or two of crazy golf
Keep missing those little holes
Fish and chips and mushy peas
Eaten with a wooden fork
A drink in a seaside pub
Listening to people talk
See The Jolly Fisherman
Take in the bracing air
Skegness on a summer's day
I wish that I were there.

Paul Duddles

MY BELOVED ISLAND
(Ellen Vannin. The Isle of Man)

My heart's on an island
Within the Irish Sea.
Away with the fairies
That's where I long to be.
Recapturing endless days
Of joy and happiness.
Holidaying amid such scenic
                              loveliness.
Sun-filled glens - flora abound
Spiked monbretia, ballerina
                    fuchsias dance around -
Everywhere. Clear-water bays
Pebbled shores and golden sand
Frame this pleasant wonderland.

I now look across from another shore
Towards this isle so fair
Wishing to rejoin my heart
That is forever captive there.

Marnie Connley

TUMMEL VALLEY

Tummel Valley far away.
The sun will shine and shine all day.
The children there will play and play
until their hearts' content.

A play park is just around the bend
with a river running near it.
People fish there with their rods,
and catch fish swimming through it.

When you leave to say goodbye,
the tears will start to fall.
But when you think of the fun you've had
it's worth it after all!

Sean McFadden (9)

OUR FAVOURITE PLACE TO BE

I think that Wales is beautiful
so does my husband too
As we both went there together
right back in '72.
We went there on our honeymoon
but couldn't afford a lot
So we brought an old red Zephyr
and tried to do it up.
First my husband cut some wood
to fit between the seats
And then I made some curtains
so no-one else could peep.
We also had a mattress
some sheets and blankets too
So we could cuddle up at night
the way most couples do.
By 6am each morning though
we both were washed and dressed
And then we lit our Primus up
to fry some sausages.
But when we both reached Brecon
we couldn't believe our eyes
As when we looked around us
we could see for many miles.
We also went to Betws-y-Coed
and Aberystwyth too
Then stopped a while in Llandudno
to take in all the view
It really was so lovely there
I bet you'd love it too.

Merilyn Gulley

THE SEA

I wish that I could see the sea
Somewhere, where I love to be
A fresh sea breeze upon my face
Salt-kissed lips I long to taste
Soft warm sand beneath my feet
Shimmering surf in summer's heat
Fond memories of holidays
Sun cream, ice cream, lazy days
I wish that I could see the sea
What a tonic that would be

Shirley

SUMMER

Open the windows, welcome the sun,
Clear are the heavens - summer's begun,
Let in the warmth of the southerly breeze,
Be wary, the pollen is making you sneeze,
Doctor's best medicine, easing your pain,
Go for a cycle ride on Salisbury Plain,
Treasure and nurse all that you hold dear,
View the long robe of a biblical seer,
Have all your friends to tea, sit by the fire,
With a musician tuning the lyre,
Open the windows, welcome the sun,
Clear are the heavens, summer's begun.

Peter Buss

BIASED VIEW

Twixt sea and downs lay Worthing
Then as now my home
Seat of all my learning
The place where I have grown
I ran her streets in childhood
In peace and during war
Explored her hills and wildwood
And played upon her shore
Travel and excitement or rest within her arms
Are offered by the borough
As part of all her charms
So visit us this summer
And take the break you're yearning
The south coast boasts no greater
Joy for holidays than Worthing

Edward J Butler

SINGING THE SONG OF JASMINE

Was it,
Only the moment's caring whisper
That flew in across the burning desert sands,
That touched me upon the shoulder
As light as a perfumed songbird,
To turn my head around;
Or perhaps,
An early opening breeze
Singing the song of jasmine across the blazoned day,
To open the first flutterings of your petalled eyelashes
Like a butterfly of the cried wing,
Over the mulberry skies for the first flower to be found;
Or was it,
Too much the burnished gold of collected sun
Against my beating heart and chest,
That brought the silent hushes of the pale moon
Upon the awakening thought, for those painted henna heavens
Of the hidden jewel were always beyond the lands of me;
And perhaps,
The shawls of emerald night just spun the song of nestling reeds
Across the morning stars and amongst life's sweetened springs
                                        of thirsting,
To ever dance the day in lighter gowns
Behind the palm-leafed shades of veil
And leading paths of dream, just to allow the memory to flow free?

Norman Royal

TOTNES, DEVON

I wish I were in Totnes
with my friend Dorothy,
in her small town cottage,
a bus ride from the sea.
In fact as I gazed at the mural
she'd painted on her garden wall,
I could swear that the waves
were real. I truly felt quite cool.
From the window I could see
green hills, placidly grazing sheep,
and the river flowing to Dartmouth.
I had the deepest sleep.
The castle stands serenely
looking down on market square,
the bustle, and the friendly chat,
on market days all flock there.
We strolled along the river bank
and in the evening sun's full glare
saw light reflected on the
boats, I was without a care.
Totnes was such a friendly place,
I felt at home there right away,
but all too soon the week had flown
and I woke to my final Totnes day.
I can't wait to return to Totnes
and my friend Dorothy,
to see her small town cottage
and her mural of the sea.

Maisie Dance

A Favourite Place

As soon as the summer sun shines down
Airports are crammed as folk leave town.
But those crowded places are not for me,
For I have a place of sweet memory.
It is one of those delightful spots,
Old cottages, boats and lobster pots,
A picture straight from a chocolate box.
Only one road leads in, it is sheltered, cocooned,
And in lush green hills you become marooned.
This beautiful cove casts a spell on the mind,
You instantly leave worries and troubles behind.
Unspoilt, and nothing to do but laze,
Or potter among rock-pools in a sun-soaked haze,
Smiling at babes paddling in the ripple-tide sand,
First exciting adventure clutching mother's hand.
So little has changed with the passing of time,
A warp where everything remains sublime.
There is still the same little rock-cleft shack
To walk for a cup of tea and back,
And children still content to stand for eons
Choosing flavours of ice cream for their cones.
When it's time to leave, you glance back at this space
And suddenly the world seems a better place,
And you think to yourself, this piece of Devon
God surely dropped straight down from heaven.

But now I sit entrapped with age
Dreaming from my gilded cage
Of that place of quiet serenity
So full of youthful memory -
And that is where I'd like to be.

Irene Locke

SEASIDE MORNING - LOWESTOFT, SUFFOLK

A thrill of exhilaration, allusive, and fleeting,
A lilting thing, of happiness, along the esplanade,
A blue sky morning feel, with summertime delighting,
as evening lanterns throw their elongated shades
along the ways of paddle pool and pier.

And down below, the beach of limpid sea ashine,
with the sun about to rise above, the horizontal line,
along the eastern sky, of morning haze and dawn
as the jellyfish are stranded, with tired waves
withdrawn, across the sands, of time and sea.

And seafront small hotels, with 'vacancies' in windows,
facing outwards to the east, of esplanade and pier,
with beach towels on the windowsills
and buckets in front porches, and slung between
the seafront lamps, - festoons of multicoloured bulbs
that cast their shadows on last night's farewells.

Walter Gilder

WHEN THE SUN SHINES

When the sun shines the best place to be
Is Britain, there's so many places to see
Fields of green and leafy lanes
You'll want to walk again and again

Scotland's lochs are black and deep
Lomond, is that where old Nessie creeps
In the glens it's quiet and still
Glorious heather's on the hill

A trip to the Isle of Skye
Its beauty brings a tear to the eye
Lonely sheep wander and graze
Round crofters' cottages of bygone days

Coal mines in Wales where hard work was done
Mountains of slack are warmed by the sun
Ffestiniog railway runs up and on
In wonderful Wales, land of song

The Garden of Eden, Kent is renowned
For Canterbury Cathedral where kings were crowned
Castles and keeps strong and fine
Stonework and ancestry weathered by time

Fossils can be found on Cornwall's rocky coast
Glorious beaches of which locals can boast
Pretty thatched cottages with low oak beams
Dartmoor ponies, outcrops and streams

Walk through woods and over stiles
Streams meander for miles and miles
Sit on a log, take a rest
Watch the sun setting down in the west

Pamela A Smith

WHERE I'D LIKE TO BE

It's summertime and the birds are singing,
The sun is scorching my face,
It's too hot.

I'd like to be up on a mountain,
Where the breeze is fresh and cool,
I could see the whole world from a mountain top,
And then I could shout 'I rule!'

I'd like to be deep in a forest,
The shade makes me cool you see,
If quiet I could see foxes and squirrels,
But most likely they'd first see me.

I'd like to be at the bottom of the ocean,
And see all the wonders down there,
The dolphins could swim and play with me,
And fish could swim through my hair!

Sharon Davies (13)

HOLIDAYS

If I went on holiday,
To a country far away,
I wouldn't care if it was hot or cold,
Or even if the streets were paved with gold,
'Cause if I didn't have my family with me,
I'd be as bored as can be.

So if I stayed here in Wales,
To spend my holiday in rain and gales,
I'd be content in my caravan,
Getting no summer tan,
Just with my family having fun,
And who cares if we never see the sun.

Joanna Mogford (14)

BANK HOLIDAYS

Let's get out the deck chairs
Kick off shoes and laze,
Cool drinks on the table,
Enjoy the sunny days,
Only noise the bumble-bees
Humming round the flowers,
Off we'll doze in sun-soaked bliss,
We could lay here for hours.

Who wants to sit in traffic jams?
In hot and stuffy car,
Then have to find a parking spot,
We're happy where we are,
So let's slap on the sun cream
And have a stress-free day,
Enjoying our home comforts
In our garden hideaway.

Irene Carter

HOME GROUND

Inside the grey weather-beaten walls
Lies my heavenly haven

Beneath these old craggy walls
Tangled webs of mature rose bushes
Multiple sprays finely sculptured
Yet cloaking a host of razor thorns

Sprinkled along the border
Rooted in crumbly sweet-smelling soil
Bloom flowers from many nations
Heads laden with rich pollen
Cordial breeze carries heady fragrances
Across slim affluent grass

Within this verdant growth
The elderly oak tree holds court
Generous branches spread-eagled to sapphire sky
In salutation to a fiery July sun

Below this natural lattice ceiling
I scribble and dream
Sheltered in my castle of tranquillity
No daggers of distraction
Only nature's sweet melodies
To serenade my mind

If only summer was immortal
Or minutes became hours
Then would I be contented
To while away a season or two
Here in my garden

D A Watson

SUMMER MOMENT

Coming to the swampy edge
water squelches warm
between my bare toes.

Cast-aside clothes form a trail
till in absolute freedom,
I head for the deeps.

Icy water makes me gasp
as it clutches
at goose-pimpled flesh.

Afloat, weightless I let the lake claim me.
Sunlight pours down,
piercing brown water.

Golden limbs shimmering
I melt, liquefy;
even my skin sings.

Betty Tindal

MY GARDEN

There is no finer place for me,
Than to sit in my garden,
Under the willow tree.
The sun beats down,
Upon the ground.
And flowers in profusion all around.
I love their colours, perfume and hue.
God put them there for us to view.

And when I have sat there for a while.
I snooze and wake up with a smile.
I remember the Lord has given me the skill.
To place those lovely flowers,
Arranged in a vase upon my windowsill.

Susan B Marlow

A TROPICAL DREAM

What would you say
If I took you away
To a land in a tropical sea

Where the sun burns so strong
On sands golden and long
And eat fruit from the coconut tree

Our days spent in bliss
The nights sealed with a kiss
As I hold you tight in my arms

With the moon we would dine
As the stars glitter and shine
Making love under whispering palms

But these are just dreams
Of faraway themes
When your world is a dark empty cave

But we can go there
For dreams are to share
Let's drift away on a tropical wave

Terry White

BRANCASTER BEACH, NORTH NORFOLK

Golden sun on golden sand
Blue sea caresses quiet the land.
Storms of winter now all passed
Summertime is here at last.

Seashells spangle on the shore
Soft wind's touch adds warm allure.
Golden path to setting sun
Shimmering when day is done.

Silver beams from moon on high
Crystal stars in velvet sky.
Silent swirl of satined waves
As turquoise to the dawn does pave.

Ah! Brancaster - when truth I tell
It's June, there's rain and sleet as well!
White horses foam on cold grey sea
Sandstorm from dunes does blow round me.

Yet I love with all my heart
North Norfolk coast where I did start.
And when this life does end for me
Cast my ashes off Brancaster into the sea.

Anita Richards

THE RIVER AT CAMBRIDGE

I went to Cambridge one summer's day
To punt on the river so relaxing to lay
There in a boat green grass either side
Slowly up river the boat gently glides
Our hands trailed the water so calm
I laid so softly there in your arms.
A day on the river in water serene
A beautiful place that you've ever seen
The sun cast its shadows there on the wall
While overhead trees stood upright and tall
I'll go back to Cambridge one summer's day
To punt on the river and in a boat lay.

Thelma Hynes

HOLIDAYS

The sun is shining
It's very hot
I think I'll find
A shady spot
To sit and rest
And if I can
I'll get myself
A nice suntan.
In time, I'll build
A big sandcastle
And in amongst
The waves I'll battle
I'll jump and leap
Then back to shore
Lie back, relax
And sleep some more.
Oh lazy times
No cares my way
If only life was always
A holiday!

Karen Jones

WHERE I LOVE TO BE

I sit in my garden and look around,
At all my family:
The sun is shining on every one of us,
Oh, what a wonderful day for me.

Bill, my husband, looking after each one,
And relaxed in each garden chair
Is Jennifer and Alex and Margaret and Jim,
Even my son, Anthony is there.

There's Jason and Lucy, both eighteen,
And fifteen-year old Adam I see,
How lovely that we are all together,
But the happiest person, is me.

I love the sun, no doubt about that,
But even if it wasn't there:
My favourite place is with my family,
Because life together we all share.

Dorothy Whitehall

A Late Summer Afternoon

Pale fresh air
sweet warmth
gentle, clean, soft, relaxed

Floating thin clouds
late sun glow
peace of mind
a beautiful feeling

Calm and sleepy
a feeling of love
then the sky shows a glimmer
a glimmer of what's above.

James Slater

Sussex

When traffic fumes bounce garden wall
And spoil the balmy evenings' call,
When city dust invades my space
I yearn to leave the human race
And hie away to woods and weald,
Commune with sheep content in field,
Sky search for rooks in far-off trees
And feel the touch of summer breeze.

Oh, not for me heat-hazy sands
Or sunburnt shores of foreign lands
I to the hills, an ardent rover
Tread tufty paths of moss and clover
Stretch limbs, and breathe the salty air
Cast off the urban life of care,
Behold from downs the distant sea,
Refresh my soul and set it free.

Marion P Webb

CARIBBEAN CALYPSO

Come a strollin' man
Come a strollin' wid me
Come a strollin' man
Till we see de coconut tree

Steel drum sound at break of day
For carnival that on its way
An' people sit in de palm tree light
As people show-off de costumes bright

Come a strollin' man
Come a strollin' wid me
Come a strollin' man
Till we see de coconut tree

Salt fiiish an' pomerac fresh today
Or passion fruit from de bay
De coconuts fresh an' ready to eat
In me liddle barrow today

Come a strollin' man
Come a strollin' wid me
Come a strollin' man
Till we see de coconut tree

People come at end of day
An' do a dance to Caribbean sway
An' people dress in more costumes bright
As people dance all thro' de night

Come a strollin' man
Come a strollin' wid me
Come a strollin' man
Till we see de coconut tree.

Christopher Johnson (10)

BONNIE SCOTLAND

Some people travel over the world,
To far and distant shores.
To islands with strange sounding names,
Like the Caymans or Azores.
A paradise on earth,
Is what they hope to find.
Too blind to see the beauty,
Of the land they leave behind.

For here in Bonnie Scotland,
From John O' Groats to the Solway Firth.
Is a land of rugged beauty,
And it's mine by right of birth.
The mountains in the highlands,
Where the air is pure and free.
Or the Coolins on the Isle of Skye,
Are places I love to be.

To walk among the heather,
Watch the eagle soaring high.
Rest in a peaceful glen,
Whilst time ticks slowly by.
So you can holiday abroad,
In New York or in Rome.
But I will spend my summer,
In this land that is my home.

M Muirhead

THE BEAUTY OF BEACHES

The best place to be,
Is by the sea,
When the sun is shining,
And the temperature climbing.

Take a book to read,
And some sun cream you'll need,
Find a good spot,
Where it's nice and hot!

Lay back and relax,
And enjoy to the max!
If it's warm, take a dip,
If it's not, this I'd skip!

Take a walk by the shore,
So at lunch you'll eat more,
Then afternoon napping,
With waves gently lapping.

Ice creams to keep cool,
It's 99s that rule!
For on a summer's day,
It's at the beach you should stay!

C Shadwell

THE LAND OF THE PORTUGUESE

I stayed in the land of the Portuguese
A land of cork and almond trees,
A land of blossoms, colours rare
Eucalyptus scents the air,
In the land of the Portuguese.

Little old ladies, black adorned
Colours bright, long ago scorned,
Widowed young but still staunch and true
In their weeds, they accept their due
In the land of the Portuguese.

Friendly people by the score
Sit outside their family door,
In tiny mountain villages high
Cast a wave to passers-by,
In the land of the Portuguese.

Figs abundant on the hills,
Oranges, lemons from land untilled,
Bursting pomegranates red and gay,
Send down their seeds in bright array
In the land of the Portuguese.

Ada Ferguson

HOLIDAYS

Holidays are exciting . . . discover all things new
Enjoyed by many . . . not just the chosen few

Prospect of finding . . . new places to explore
To live in dreams . . . never lived in before

Savouring traditions . . . like food and wine
Being able to chat . . . taking ages to dine

Home and . . . not just cases you hold
Memories etched . . . and stories to be told

Archie Grant

DREAM HOLIDAY

I dream of a sun-washed island
Far away above the clouds
Away from familiar places
A veritable paradise!

My sweetheart as companion
Through orange-grove, shady vine,
We'd wander blissful - no disruption
In a heaven all our own.

In outer-space we'd topsy-turvy
Flying angels in a 'novel scene',
Maybe visit other islands
Where no earthman's ever been.

Heavenly sun-kissed imagination
But oh the 'bliss' . . . as one pretends,
'Space-borne' lifts a flight of fancy
So why not dream, Poetic Friends!

Mary Skelton

THE SMELL OF SUMMER

The season of summer is a happy season full of joy and laughter.
With children playing all around having a good time.
With the colour of the flowers that look so beautiful
with their scent that fills the air.
With plants and bushes that look so green and
trees so tall that bear fruit.
With the smell of freshly cut grass.
With the birds singing and playing.
With the bees busy buzzing around doing their thing
With nature so wild and free.
In the peaceful forest where the sun shines through
From the sky so blue.

C J Walls

SUMMERTIME

In the summer
I love to stay
At home in my garden
And catch some rays

The beach is also
A wonderful place
To get a tan
And a smile on your face

Wherever you are
I'm sure you'll agree
With your family and friends
Is the best place to be.

Natalie Coleman (13)

WISH YOU WERE HERE

Wish you were here, this lovely day
To share with me the countryside,
But you have gone a life away
You left me when you died.

Wish you were here at life's crossway
To point the path to roam
But I am left alone to stray,
Along the path to home.

Yet you are still within my heart,
The mistle-thrush defies the rain.
The eyes you opened play their part
And we hold hands in 'Memory Lane'.

John Hope Urwin

HOLIDAYS

I love to lie on a sun-drenched beach
With a long cool drink, just at arms reach,
I love the sights and sounds of Spain,
Instead of the constant drip of rain.
I love to bathe in warm blue sea,
This beautiful land is like heaven to me.
The people are slow and kind,
Do as you please, no one will mind
Nobody worries, no stress or strife.
But everyone has a real passion for life.
If I had my way,
Here's where I'd stay,
But I have to return,
I've a living to earn.

June V Johnson

THE GARDEN CENTRE

As I sit and look around,
The sun is shining down,
All around the ground,

I see the flowers out in bloom,
Knowing that it will be
    summer soon,
There's all different colours around,
And so much joy to be found,

The wind it is a-blowing,
Flowing softly through the trees,
It is so very nice to feel,
This early summer breeze,

As people are just walking by,
Feeling the summer sun from
    above the sky,
Looking at the lovely flowers
    in bloom,
At the garden centre in the month
    of June,

It's peaceful just sitting here,
With my glass of sparkling water,
Not sitting on my own,
But with Hayley my daughter,

So the next time you visit this
    garden centre,
Take in the peace and comfort too,
Knowing that you will be fulfilled,
In everything that you do.

Jessica Wright

AT THE SEASIDE - SKEGNESS

With my bucket and spade,
I don't need a parade,
Only Skegness is the place for me.
A place on the beach, ice cream. Whoopee!

My little heart pounds,
As my feet tread the grounds.
Warm sands awashing my toes.
Superb! Fantastic! Here goes.

I find a good spot.
Sheltered, not too hot.
And put cream on my body and face,
As I don't want to burn.

On this special day,
With so many castles to make,
I make quite a lot.
With flags on the top.

And paper for windows, and doors,
They look almost real,
Elegant! Grandeal!
Even 'Beau Geste', would applaud.

Michael John Swain

Dawn In A Summer Meadow

Butterfly shadows hover and play, touching the moss and the reed,
Sunlight on water reflects in the eye, as pearls on the cobwebs recede.

Dawn is the time for nature to wake, the time of the day often missed,
By mortals like us, still covered by down, instead of the soft
gentle mist.

Very occasionally we stir in our sleep, and wander abroad at this hour,
In the silence and softness of each breaking day, we witness the strength
of its power.

The sound of awakening of insects and birds, each only the sound of
a pin,
But combined close together, by a million times, the silence becomes
a great din.

Nature permits us to share in this rite, and repeats it day after day,
But man without wisdom, ignores the vast sight, and pushes the
wonder away.

Janet Allen

NANT Y MOCH

Turn from the main road on this warm summer day
Leave behind lorries of wood and hay
On all sides are mountains towering high
Wand'ring sheep run as we pass by
A view of the dam's majestic wall
Overhead hear a curlew call
A rock-scattered beach, a huge sparkling lake
From trickling streams its waters intake
Ancient mountains rise up from the edge
Waves run through the paddling sedge
Acres of conifers giving cool shade
Green sphagnum moss is brightly arrayed
It's so relaxing so quiet and free
There's a wealth of natural life to see
Remote and wild, this beautiful scene
Always remains wherever you've been
The mountains don't change as time moves on
But man-made things will all soon be gone
Uplifting, tranquil, unhurried peace
These small lapping waves will never cease
Life carries on, the seasons move
But this rural scene you couldn't improve
People will rush and lorries will crawl
But the Cambrian mountains will outlive them all.

Wendy Dedicott

PARADISE IN THE SUMMER

I'm stuck here, in my garden shed,
tending to my tomatoes lying in their tomato bed.
I feel down and out, getting restless all the time,
all hot and sweaty, with my glass of wine.
I sit down perched upon a sticky wooden stool,
wanting to be somewhere else, somewhere nice and cool.
Then I drift into my thoughts, my thought wonderland,
I wonder where I could be, perhaps on the sand.
I know, a tropical island, yes, that is where I would be,
not a person in sight, in the middle of the sea.
My own little paradise, to do what I will,
palm trees all around me, so perfectly still.
Walking down the beach, which is beautifully white,
the sun shining on my face, so vast and so bright.
And when night-time comes, a gentle breeze is stirred,
I lie on my bed of leaves as I listen to a little bird.
A cocktail in one hand, and in the other rests a flower,
time passing by and a minute seems like an hour.
With all being peaceful, my eyelids begin to fall,
my eyes get so very tired and I hear the animal kingdom call.
But then I'm brought back to reality, which seems so very plain,
and I'm tending to my tomatoes in their bed again.

Kerry Hayley (16)

SUMMERTIME

The sun comes out another day is upon me
I glance out of the window
I see children playing and having fun
I now know summertime has come

People walk past me with happy faces
leaving traces of tropical scent behind them
I now know summertime has come.

I look at my watch it's half-past nine at night
and is still light outside
Me and my friends laugh and chat away about the
things we like best

I walk up the road I hear the cars passing by
playing summer music tunes
I hum along to it because I know it's one of my favourites
it puts a smile upon my face
I now know it's summertime

I look at the flowers as they blossom out in people's gardens
reminds me of the colours of the rainbow
they smell so sweet
After all I now know it's summertime.

Katherine Ring (17)

COLOURS OF THE WEST

Rust-red earth and green-gold cider,
Thick cream, as yellow as butter.
Purple-flamed sunsets reflected in streams,
Colours of the west, colours of our dreams.

Ice cream houses of pink, white and lemon,
Huddle around ochre-red sands.
Cream-frilled waves, whipped-up on the wind
Colours of the west, colours in the mind.

Dancing boats of every hue, nudge in harmony,
Slate-grey fish lie on silver-white ice,
Whilst yellow-beaked gull, wails and cries.
Colours of the west, reflections in the eyes.

H McQuirke

SAFE HAVEN FOR THE SPIRITUAL WARRIOR (SOULMATES)

There's a sun-drenched desert island,
With a tree-lined sandy shore.
Three mountains at its centre,
And a lake of mystical blue.

In a rocky cove,
Three dolphins dance serenely
Safe from mankind's stupid ignorance
They really do entrance.

In the untouched shady forests,
Live the animals, free to run.
Safe from mankind's foolish greed,
They truly live in peace.

Beneath the calming waters,
Live all the creatures of the sea.
They live in safe tranquillity,
On a wondrous coral reef.

It is my own safe haven,
A place where I can go,
To receive some inner healing,
Peace and lasting calm.

Whenever I am sad and low
I just sit quiet, rest, relax,
And wait for my guide to take me
To the place that I call, safe haven.

Our inner-selves, know what we need.
To live life peacefully.
That's why, when we really need some help,
We find our hidden key

Arion

KORCULA: VISTAS OF A DALMATIAN HOLIDAY

The end of the peninsula swells
Into a red-roofed town
Billowing upwards to its cathedral
Whose tall tower clears the nestling mound.
Sunlight smoothes rounded bastion
And softens crenellation;
While rooftops rutilate,
Trees girdle the town with coolness.
Boats approach from every angle,
Scudding or chugging across the bay.
Human heads are dotting the sea,
Busy about their holiday.
Relaxation, pleasure-in-being
Extends its outstretched fingers.

Mount the steps to the old town:
Balconies, archways, pediments, alcoves -
Architectural details swarm
Though in restricted space.
Mellow yellow greying stone -
Pledge of lasting beauty -
Radiates serenity,
A silent guardian spirit.

Beyond the city vistas the Maquia evolves.
Undulating pines and wispy cypresses try to clothe
The hills whose bare rock would repulse them.
Olive trees glisten grey in the valleys,
And grapes hang green above earth like dried blood;
Amidst the bleached scrubland seedheads of wild flowers seethe;
On lusher hills green and purple kaleidoscope through all the shades.
Nature unspoilt calms the complicated mind.

Anne Sanderson

THE CELTIC PRINCE

The city in summer encases me,
Chokes me,
With claustrophobic chaos.
That's when,
Dressed in robes of velvet green,
The Celtic Prince calls.
Across the sea he sits and waits;
My soul's ancient lover.
Here, in the dirt and the smoke,
His stories speak to me.
But only there, can I freely dance
Along orange and red embroidery
Of his gown's flowing hem.
Or roll through the Connemaran curves
Of his slender fingers,
And watch his cousin, the sun
Flicker over the western sea.
From here, I can hear his cries of pain
Inflicted by thorns recently forced
Onto his delicate head.
From here, I wince.
Only there can I comfort and be comforted.
I hear his lilting voices beckoning me
To come and be wrapped in his arms,
And soothed to eternal peace.

Elaine Carter

EASTBOURNE

Ozone, fragrant breath of sea
Happy sunburnt faces
Leaving behind reality
Worries leave line traces.

Every day enjoy
Look and look around you
As your senses you employ
Enjoying now and déjà vu.

Relaxing, lazing, dreaming
Remembering times gone by
Planning daily, scheming
To enjoy each day you try.

And the sunshine is warming
And it's nice to be waited upon
And the sea view is exciting
And who's here when you've gone.

The seagulls scream a welcome
You've come again this year
And when it's time to say goodbye
You'll brush away a tear.

Red arrows swooping, diving
Seaside business easily thriving
Flowered carpets growing well
Even flowers caught in the spell.

Sun is shining every day
Rain at night so they say
The pier is long and full of life
Smiling people who've banished strife

My once a year to Eastbourne's gone
But next year we've another one . . .

Anne Clark

JOYS OF SUMMER

Golden sunshine for to see
Glorious times there's so much glee.
Flourishing blooms bringing delight
A blaze of colour this wondrous sight.
Summer joys for all to share
Happiness, splendour everywhere.
Family outings such laughter gay
Picnic pleasures to enjoy alway.
Rippling waters ebb and flow
Silver white sands forever glow.
Countryside strolls - such peace restore
Tranquil moments we all do adore.

Margaret Jackson

SUNNY HUNNY (HUNSTANTON)

My favourite place in summer is Sunny Hunny,
That's where I like to spend some money.
We took the caravan to the camping site,
There we enjoyed barbecues or a party night.
I played bingo, so quiet not even a sound,
Hoping to be lucky and win a round.
A walk on the beach, then take off my shoes,
Remove the sand from out of my toes.
I sit on a deck chair with a nice cup of tea,
And watch children paddling in the sea.
Then a stroll in the gardens to see the flowers,
They were a picture after welcome showers.
I relax on a seat,
To rest my weary feet.
For tea I had the tasty bits,
A nice plate of fish and chips.
A visit to the amusement park,
Before it began to get dark,
A game on the slot machines,
Waiting for pennies to drop,
A coin was lodged in the slot,
So we couldn't win a lot.
A walk along the promenade in the evening sun,
Then to the Princess Theatre before the show had begun.
After the show we walk back to the caravan,
For a good night's rest,
This is Sunny Hunny at its best.
A favourite holiday resort on the east coast
There's a wide variety of shops in the town,
Some prices are high others cause a frown.

Margery English

I'D RATHER BE

It's the beginning of July,
You're sat in maths,
The six weeks are dawning.
You pray for the last day
But it's only Monday morning.

You've been set some homework that has to be done
But you're just thinking of six weeks in the sun.
You start to dream
About a holiday in Jamaica or Spain,
But the more you think about it
The more you drive yourself insane.

Just think!
Blue sea, a hot bright sun
All the fun.
Long walks along the beach
In shorts and T-shirts.

On TV it looks so cool,
But at the moment you're sat in maths
And remember this year you're only
Going to Blackpool.

Leanne Hall (14)

SUMMER'S DAY

On a hot summer's day,
When it's humid and hot,
I long to be by the sea.

The earth is baked dry,
Plants wither, turn brown,
On a hot summer's day.

Windows are open, we long for a wind,
Skin is sweaty, perspiration on brow.
I long to be by the sea.

Butter is rancid, cold water is warm,
Tempers short, children squabble, complain,
On a hot summer's day.

The office is stifling, nerves are frazzled,
Sun is bright through the window, burning the eyes.
I long to be by the sea.

The dog is panting, greenflies sit on leaves,
Flowers, desperate for water, leaves yellow and drooped.
On a hot summer's day,
I long to be by the sea.

Dorothea Carroll

MEDITERRANEAN MEDALLION

Tideless water, softly lapping,
Rippled, rockless, beige-white sand.
Silver dome on hillside glistening,
Church towers dominate, command . . .

'Lift your eyes up, see my glory.
Here I stand, and every day
My majestic presence draws you
From the tranquil turquoise bay.'

Gazing up from lazy torpor,
Bathing, floating, so at ease
Cooling sea and scorching sunshine,
Imagining people on their knees.

Many tempting things on offer,
Cheesecake, pasta, prickly pear
Filigree of gold and silver,
Candles, glass and tableware.

Memories of sunblest childhood
In this place the happiest . . .
Shallow water, deep aroma
Sand, by saline froth caressed.

Malta! Independent island
Proud and fortress-like display,
All your history, all your grandeur,
But let me swim in Mellieha Bay!

Heather A Hayne

CHILDHOOD MEMORY

A small brick wall opened the door,
Childhood confusion led me on.
Nature has reclaimed this plot,
Fragments of an orchard were left.
Sugar babies caused summer snow,
Parents wished them away.
Weeds were deep and dense as any sea
Making you feel colourful,
Rich and free.
I waded through nettle stings and bruises
With a blackbird in hand.
For fun apple trees were climbed.
As I surveyed the ground around
I could own everything I could see.
Below soil broken blue glass was
Unearthed.
Now this plot is long gone,
As man-made development moves
On.

Lorraine Johns

OLD BINOCULARS

It was a day for porpoises, smooth
backs rising and falling in the waves.
When the white sail'd dinghies
tacked out to sea, the bay was theirs,
a playground ocean, washing in velvet crabs with
monstrous eyes. Rock pools a child's paradise.
I will never tire of this place, this Devon coastline,
wind whistling over the cliff, grass bending flat
without a footfall. Yellowhammers like feathered suns
on the bush, against a cobalt sky.
Fleetingly a whitethroat, perches on spiny gorse,
thrift pink on jagged rock, bobbing in the breeze, that
holds the skylark's song.
Everything, so sharp today through the old binoculars
that rarely were. Watching intently, hill crest suddenly
broken, by swift, silent wings swooping low
on reconnaissance, so close! And up, up, out toward
the headland, the peregrine's talons empty . . .

Jacquie L Smith

WOODLAND RAMBLE

When e'er a fine summer day has risen,
And the glory of the sun awakes the
woodland denizen;
Oft' I will ramble a narrow lane whose
woodlands arise to winged lyres,
And butterflies flutter among the
blossom laden briars.
And to hear so sweet, oh so gay,
A skylark heralds the rising day.
The chatty brook calls to the
bowing willow,
And fleecy clouds above shady
bowers billow.
The birds are jolly in the hedge,
A dormouse wanders the waving sedge;
The dunnock rears a crafty cuckoo
to her nest,
A bold robin perches on his twiggy
rest.
And when in solitude I seek to find
the wonders of nature's trail,
And to hear with joyous rapture the
song of a nightingale.

Peter Morriss

KENT IN SUMMER

Little Katie liked to stay on Kentish sward
here in the garden of England.
Explored, when visiting from Yorkshire moor
flowered hilltops and seashore, each summer.

With saucy smiles and nimble feet
skipping through waves - gave each heart a treat,
as aunt Joanne joined in, with merry prance
seagulls' raucous cry, applauded the dance.

The magic of a summer holiday
creating memories pot-pourri, of childhood sweet,
to soon melt like ice cream in the heat.
When autumn leaves float down - remember,
               a Kentish summer daisy crown . . .

Joanne Manning

WOODLAND GARDEN

Designed for you - by me - helped by many,
I wanted to share my vision,
My dream,
I wanted a perfect solution.

In a world of competition, I wanted peace,
For you a gift.
Co-operation,
Time to reflect, in harmony.

Nature understood my aim,
We worked as one,
A team,
Our gift, your world, respect it!

Yvonne Wilkinson

INFORMATION

We hope you have enjoyed reading this book - and that you will continue to enjoy it in the coming years.

If you like reading and writing poetry drop us a line, or give us a call, and we'll send you a free information pack.

Write to :-
**Triumph House Information
1-2 Wainman Road
Woodston
Peterborough
PE2 7BU
(01733) 230749**